If you were a

Noun

by Michael Dahl ~ illustrated by Sara Gray

PICTURE WINDOW BOOKS
Minneapolis, Minnesota

noun (n) a word that names a person, place, or thing

Editor: Christianne Jones
Designer: Nathan Gassman
Page Production: Tracy Kaehler
Creative Director: Keith Griffin
Editorial Director: Carol Jones
The illustrations in this book were created
with acrylics.

Picture Window Books
151 Good Counsel Drive
P.O. Box 669
Mankato, MN 56002-0669
877-845-8392
www.picturewindowbooks.com

Printed in the United States of America.

**Library of Congress
Cataloging-in-Publication Data**
Dahl, Michael.
If you were a noun / by Michael Dahl ;
illustrated by Sara Gray.
p. cm. — (Word fun)
Includes bibliographical references
and index.
ISBN-13: 978-1-4048-1355-7 (hardcover)
ISBN-10: 1-4048-1355-1 (hardcover)
ISBN-13: 978-1-4048-1980-1 (paperback)
ISBN-10: 1-4048-1980-0 (paperback)
1. English language—Noun—Juvenile
literature. 1. Gray, Sara, ill. II. Title.
III. Series.

PE1201.D34 2006
428.1—dc22   2005021854

Special thanks to our advisers for their expertise:
Rosemary G. Palmer, Ph.D., Department of Literacy, College of Education, Boise State University
Susan Kesselring, M.A., Literacy Educator, Rosemount–Apple Valley–Eagan (Minnesota) School District

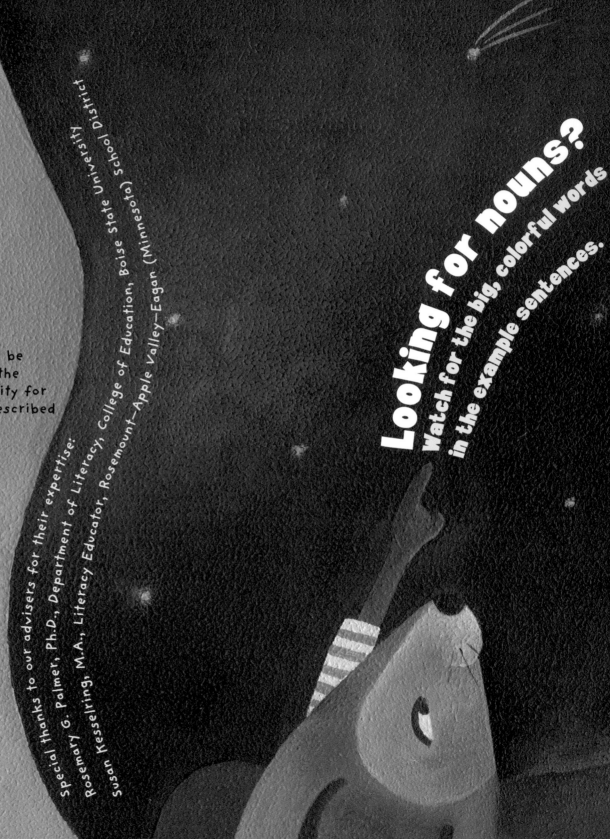

Looking for nouns?

Watch for the big, colorful words
in the example sentences.

If you were a noun ...

3

... you would be

a **STAR**,

a **CLOUD**,

4

an ASTRONAUT, or the MOON.
Let's blast off into the world of nouns!

If you were a noun, you would be easy to spot. You would be a person, a place, or a thing.

You could be an ASTRONAUT

preparing to fly into SPACE in a SPACESHIP.

If you were a noun, you could be proper. A proper noun is a specific person, place, or thing. The first letter of a proper noun is always capitalized.

A rocket flies out of Cape Canaveral in Florida.

Names are proper nouns, so they are always capitalized.

The first astronaut to walk on the moon was Neil Armstrong.

If you were a noun, you could be a single thing. A noun that is one thing is a singular noun.

10

You could be one ALIEN with one EYE and one TENTACLE.

If you were a noun, you could be more than one thing. A noun that is more than one thing is a plural noun. Some nouns change from singular to plural by adding an "s" to the end.

12

If you were a noun, you might change your shape. Some singular nouns have to change their shape when they become plural nouns.

GALAXY becomes GALAXIES.

MOUSE becomes MICE.

WOMAN becomes WOMEN.

15

If you were a noun, you might look the same whether you were a singular or a plural noun.

one **FISH**

two **FISH**

seven **FISH**

How many fish do you see?

17

If you were a noun, you might have more than one way to describe yourself. Some things have more than one plural noun to describe them.

Clouds of space gas and dust are NEBULAS or NEBULAE.

Small, cool stars
are **RED DWARFS**
or **RED DWARVES.**

If you were a noun, you could be a group or a collection of things. You would be a collective noun.

You could be a CREW of astronauts,

a CONSTELLATION of stars,

a **SWARM** of meteors,

or a **COLONY** of space pioneers.

21

You could grow, expand, and never stop. You could become an infinity of universes ...

... if you were a noun!

The NOUN GAME

This is a guessing game to be played with a group of people.

Directions: Have each person think of a noun. Next, have each person pick three words to describe the noun. For example, if a person picked an "ice cube," he or she would say, "I am frozen, hard, and slick." Take turns guessing each person's noun.

Fact: If you look up a noun in the dictionary, you will see the letter "n" next to it. The "n" stands for noun.

Glossary

colony—a group

constellation—a group of stars that seem to form a pattern or picture

galaxy—a large group of billions of stars, planets, and other matter like dust and gas

infinity—time without end

meteor—a chunk of metal or stone that [fa]lls from space; it's also called a [sh]ooting star

nebulas—huge, bright clouds of gas and dust found in space

pioneers—people who are the first to try new things

red dwarfs—small, cool stars

swarm—a moving crowd

tentacles— long, thin body parts on some animals

universe—everything that exists, including the planets, the stars, and all of space

[Lea]rn More

At [the Lib]rary

Cle[ary, Brian] P. *A Mink, a Fink, a Skating Rink: What Is* [a noun?] [Mi]nneapolis: Carolrhoda Books, 1999.

Hei[nrichs, Ann.] *Nouns.* Chanhassen, Minn.: Child's World, [2003.]

Pulver, Ro[bin.] *Nouns and Verbs Have a Field Day.* New Y[ork: Ho]liday House, 2006.

On the Web

FactHound offe[rs a] safe, fun way to find Internet sites related to th[i]s book. All of the sites on FactHound have be[e]n researched by our staff.

1. Visit www.facthound.com
2. Type in this special code: 1404813551
3. Click on the FETCH IT button.

Your trusty FactHound will fetch the best sites for you!

Index

Look for all of the books in the Word Fun series